WHY?

WHY?

Hilde Oleson

To order additional copies of this book, contact:
Xlibris
1-888-795-4274
www.Xlibris.com
Orders@Xlibris.com
742490

CONTENTS

Acknowledgement

There are people in your life that make life difficult. There are people in my life that made my dreams possible. I would like to thank those who have sustained me, propped me up, inspired me, as I walked this new road that opened before me in my old age. Christie Andresen, who has been my true right hand, Sowmya Rao and David Morgan who appeared at the right moment to start the process, and the others who gave me food, clothing, ideas, transportation and above all strength. Thomas Hardy, Betty Williams, Sheila Norris, Beth Chapman, Kay Porter, Ed Yaconetti, Elaine Anderson and Lorraine Kujowa, Napi and Helen, Ken Stone, Nancy Griffen, Elizabeth Zeldin. And always Jeff.

Here comes the day

Here comes the day.
The dark sky is moving over. Light is moving in,
My brain stirs too.
I feel you, life, even though I do not know my destiny.
I feel a push, a thrust, a drag of my reluctant self
That would prefer to linger long in bed.
Those slanting rays that push themselves into a sky
That ruled our moods, indeed the world itself,
A few moments ago. Now the timid rays are making change.
The heavy purple grey moves back
from fronds of palest yellow
Just before I see a band of pink.
How does it dare? That timid band of pink
Against a sky so big, so foreboding?
Yet even as I watch a hand reaches down and stirs the sky
Making the horizon an orange glow
Imaginary trees and mountains loom against the clouds
Who without protest give their places up,
Again pink makes its move. And now a band of rose
Cleaves into muddy sky, spreading like wings across the wind,
The world becomes a joyous place.
Surrounded by beauty,
Embraced by an all-forgiving sky that drops its warmth on us
It's sleeping, unworthy citizens who do not know
Their future is written in the sky.

Recompense

I sort of believe
Well, sort of, maybe.
I kind of think, at least it crossed my mind,
I almost think that new gift,
This raucous raving of my mind,
These pushing, pulsing words that insist
On being written down, I do believe I have
Been given a gift.
After years of hushing, shushing, finger on the lips.
Children could be seen but not heard.
Told I had nothing to say, my comments were
Un-needed.
Told perhaps I should go to my room
To practice quiethood until I could control my mouth.
At last I find that my mouth can be quiet
If my fingers can type. The sounds are laid to rest on paper
Where they live a life separate from me.
The joy of writing came to me unbidden
From the mouths of strangers
Who said strange things like
"You saved my life". "I never knew there were others",
"Your poems helped me through a rough patch".
I never knew that reaching out through words
Could match the human soul and yet it is
A part of this strange gift that I believe,
At least I guess, perhaps is recompense for all the years before.

The need to know

They tell me I do not need to know
But Oh. I do.
I was born thirsty, always wanting to know.
They told me how and when but
Never Why.
I have now reached what has to be the closing
Chapter of my book and yet the mystery is not revealed.
I do not know Why.
Life has moved on around me.
There were days when I participated
And days when I just watched as all circled around.
I saw so many secrets revealed, stories that unwound
In silence or in screams.
I led a very ordinary life into which plunged
The extra-ordinary.
When I was drowned in misery I asked over and over
Why but no one knew.
When joy threw its gossamer mantle around me
Again I could not fathom Why I was so fortunate.
And no one knew.
Someday this life will be over. Is that the
time when I will finally learn "Why"?

Ask Why

When I was a child I was often punished
for being argumentative.
I hadn't really meant to argue
But they were grown-ups and they had the answers
And they wouldn't give them to me.
So I kept pushing, thinking I would wear them out
Until they gave up those hidden truths.
Now I know. I know I do not know
And neither did they.
What is it about the great secrets of life,
That they reveal enough to make us ask "Why",
But will not reveal the answers?
I am using up my days in useless searching.
Friends say there are no answers, but I have seen glimpses
And mechanics and scientists and rebels have seen parts.
The answers are there but so well hidden from human sight.
Could it be we are not meant to know and this desire
Will be the impetus to move us on to the next stage.
Is it possible that life is just one big Easter egg hunt,
And at the end we will be told the answers are around
The next bend? Will I go into eternity still asking "Why?"

Rhythms

When I was young
I used to rock and rock and rock.
When I'd been bad
And that was often,
My punishment was to be confined
To the old rocking chair.
How I loved it!!
Alone in my room, the rhythm matching my mood,
I rocked the hours away.
Sometimes creaking across the room
in a mad pursuit of nothing.
Other times a slow maneuver lulled passions into sleep.
Today it is the cadence of the ocean,
The waves that rock my body and my mind
Into a kind of child-like trust
That there are answers to my questions,
Solutions to my life,
The kind of rocking rhythm that permeates my life
To keep the journey going.

Going up the stairs at night

It was one of the scariest things in life.
To leave the lighted living room,
Having kissed your protector good night,
To drag your weary self to those stairs.
To look up into the dark hall ahead.
"Put on the light", your mother called.
But it is not enough.
There are dark shadows lurking.
Your feet are heavy and there is the weirdest
Sound emitting from each step.
All day you pounded up and down those stairs
Never hearing that.
It must be danger's warning.
You know there is something behind the closet door
That you must hurry past.
Light switch after switch you try to hasten
But the feet are leaden
And the fear is great.
At last, the bed. The sanctuary of the bed.
The blessed joy of crawling into bed pulling the covers tight
To find the safety of deep sleep.

Family

It started early with the morning light
Her screams lit up the morning as it had the night
Her diaper area flaming red and angry.
The boys got into a voracious fight, toppling a chair
And crying viciously.
The teakettle boiled dry, it's whistle sounding to the sky.
The day wore out, one sob after another.
At last I heard the car drive in. My husband home from work.
As he came in he stood amazed, looking at bedlam,
Hearing only cries instead of the usual joys of greeting.
He reached for me and said, "What does a man have to do
To get some peace and quiet—"
Shattered, my tears released until his arms surrounded me,
And then he said –"Oh this", and kissed me.

Work-place

Perhaps it is just a barn now,
Unused, the door for loading hay hanging
Loose banging in the wind.
But once it was a shrine.
I wandered in, eyes dim with tears
To stand at the work-bench
Where tools still held their shape,
Stayed in their orderly spots ready to be used.
Waiting to create.
The man who made his living using words
Trying to pass the gifts he felt the Lord had given him
To mortals not so closely touched by God,
That man, known to his congregations
As a messenger from God
Came here to bare his soul
He spent his time commanding these tools
Who never gave him "back-talk" as I was prone to do,
Making gifts, useful furniture,
Structures that would outlast him,
Making sure each piece was finely honed,
Built to the perfect structure,
Meeting all his qualifications as I had never done.
A workman's glove lay inert on the bench.
I picked it up and slipped it on my hand
Feeling the warmth still lingering there
"Oh, Dad," I cried, "I miss you so".

Walking on stilts

I walk on stilts through life
Afraid to come down
The world below is filled with fearful things
Up here I avoid the debris of ordinary days
Breathing the distilled air
Scented some days by the perfume of wisteria
And others by pure manure.
I know that I belong down there
Among the common souls
But long ago someone told me
I was different,
That I should find a way to separate myself
From regular people
They look up at me and smile
They do not know that though I'm in full view
I am safely hidden away
A step above, but still way down.

Answers

When winter gives up its icy grip
To let the sun warm up the sand
Then I can join the gulls to stretch out on the beach
And raise my arms so high that they
Can reach the Source.
The Source of all life's energy, the power
That moves our world and lights our lives.
We see that magic in the sun, watch every night as it turns
The darkening sky into a kaleidoscope,
Shade after shade until the blazing sun falls below the water
Leaving us forlorn and breathless.
Yet knowing in the morning it will return,
Sliding its purest rays renewed into a new-born sky
to give us hope.
High on a pole above the pier Ospreys have built a nest
Of sticks and bark, a cumbersome and rugged home
Where they will ensure the osprey heritage
Of fierce determination and strength.
When I can touch the sky, or think I can,
Another mystery unfolds. The gentle breeze becomes a storm
To lift me high and feel eternal strength,
To see the broadness of our world, the beauty where
We let nature hold forth,
The ravages where we have done our worst.
When I have seen enough I am gently put down.
Softly the sun warms me, the sand supports me,
The breeze whispers, the gulls speak and rise to
Soar above the earth, unasked for strength propelling them
To rise above us. Somewhere up there is all we need to know.
Yet I still have questions to be answered
So I will try again, trying each time to
rise a little nearer to the Source.

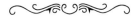

Motion Pictures

They ask me why I watch few movies.
I'd rather see life as it unrolls around me.
The fascinating actions of my neighbors,
The captured dreams of children,
The drama of the street.
The conversation overheard in the supermarket,
The furtive whispers just before the concert begins.
Is far more potent than a made up scene.
I'd rather see my grandfather steal a kiss from a blushing
Wheelchair-bound Gramdma than watch the made up passion
Of two actors who do not love each other.
The happy leaping of a dog whose sloppy
kisses are honest as it welcomes
You with meaning into its life.
So until I find the true meaning of the
mystery that surrounds me
I'll just keep watching life.

Seeking

Wandering through life
Seeking the answers
To questions unknown.
Looking each morning at the same view
Suddenly noticing
Before me a scene I have seen every day
But never truly absorbed.
All because yesterday I stumbled over a crack in the walkway
Seeing for the first time
The brave dandelion that had forced its way through concrete
To begin our spring.

Go gentle, wind.

Do you know the fear a gull feels as it plummets down
From the sky, the closing of eyes as it hits the water?
Do you know that last wild gasp as a fish joins its family
Swallowed into the gaping cavern of a whales mouth?
Can you imagine the tiny bluet that struggled
Through the dense woodland ground to bloom
As it sees a large boot hovering over it, descending, crushing?
Nature has its own desperation
I think of the goose with her very first
goslings, watching in horror as a fox
Glides in silently to snatch and run with her first born.
Our joys are so temporal, so fragile.
We hold happiness in our hands like a slim glass bowl,
Ours to protect or to shatter.

In the garden

"Look at me", screamed the sunflower.
One haughty Iris bent her head toward the pale day-lily.
"How crude", she murmured. Then pulled herself erect
As though wondering why she was
speaking to such a common flower.
She glanced down at the coral bells, tiny,
cowering silent, near the ground.
At least they know their place she said to
herself. "Not like that loud hibiscus
Flaunting her brilliance like a flag.
If they could only be like me, or even the cornflower,
Who in spite of an ordinary name stands
elegant in quiet groups".
Sage rustled in the wind. Lustrous in
the sun, she stood upright,
Her darkness sinister in the bright light.
Quietly her message seemed to spread like the sunrays over all.
"Our job", she murmurs softly, "Is to
spread beauty, not dissent."

Everything

Birds chirping madly in the tree.
Telling each other everything
You and I sitting below. holding hands.
We do not need to speak for the language of love
Flows between us.
Words, which have long meant so much to me
No longer needed.
I do not know what the birds are saying,
Cannot even interpret my heart,
Have no need.
I know you are here.

Forgive

Forgive me God
That I do not know what I want from you.
Forgive me God, if you are real,
If there really is a You.
Forgive me that I ask so much
And do not know for what I ask.
When it is granted how I hate it.
Forgive me, Life,
That when you gave me those great opportunities
I turned them down.
Forgive me Love,
That when you came I did not know you.

Alone

The trees stand stark against a glowering sky.
Last night my lover said good-bye.
The crocus that had meant to bloom was struck
By frost and falling snow.
I was laid low.
Too cold to venture out, I stand before the window
Looking out upon a world that shows no promise.
Yet to the east there is a crack of light,
A gleam of palest hope.
I stay to watch the wind push rudely at the clouds,
Hurling them from space to space,
Breaking them from groups to misty bits
That travel on alone to dissipate.
One infant cloud picks up a tint of pink.
What is there making me think solitude is good?

Bravery

In the deadness of a winter morning,
When even icicles were afraid to melt
I heard a bird singing his heart out.
Such a small bird to sing so loudly when the world
Has become so frightening.
Tsunamis, lightening strikes, first droughts, then floods
Have left us helpless.
Then there are men who strike back at that feeling.
They want to prove, at least to themselves,
That they are masters of the world.
They have to prove that they can make us cower,
That they can rule when even nature seems to turn to chaos.
But here he sings hidden in branches high enough
That we must search to find him,
But with a voice so pure and clear it fills the air.
If we can just discern his message.

Gull heart

Life contrived to keep me down
Piled trouble after pain
One tiny irritating grain of sand each day
Until there was a dune built up
Between my life and my dreams.
Years wore me down
With no reprieve from struggling or defeat
Until one day I crossed that dune
To sit beside the singing sea.
A crowd of sea gulls sat upon the sand
In a line, backs facing the sun
To absorb heat
When a large grey bird seemed to notice me
He gave an awkward squawk,
Spread out his wings, took to the air
To circle joyously, riding a current of air again and again
Effortlessly gliding down, almost landing,
Then circling again to reach that thermal carpet.
With so much envy I watched
As he rose high into the blue above
When suddenly my heart became a gull
To circle carelessly above this world
To look down on the dunes with joy.
Yes there were barriers of sand
But we could soar above them,
On the silvery wings of desire
My heart could rise with that gull.
I too could feel the heat of the sun,
The coolness of the breeze, the freedom of just being,
The bravery of circling
In a lone but beautiful sky.
Although my wings were only in my mind
I too could feel the comfort of the earth

Waiting in solid constancy below,
A place to land, to gather strength,
And then to soar again.
Within the heart of a gull.

Fly little gull

Fly little gull
Taking my heart with you.
Letting it soar over the dunes.
Fly little gull
Into the mists of morning
Seeking the sun, finding the light.
Let us lie on the strength of daylight
Knowing the day
But remembering the night.

The sorrow of it all

Grief has it's own weight
An overwhelming heaviness
Like fighting your way through
A thick but waterless fog
An intense pain that has no feeling
Dulling the senses but encumbering everything
Making every nuance of life more intense while
Rendering your feelings useless,
A tearless cry
A prayer for hope
Knowledge that nothing matters
But everything is important

Searching

What are we doing huddled here
In the darkness of our souls?
I feel your hand grip mine and yet
It does not give me strength to understand.
Is it together we must stand to know
That we are not alone?
Does it really matter—this commiserating of our minds?
We each are born alone,
Will die alone,
And make our fumbling way along the paths of life
Sometimes joining others for a while but striding off
When pleasures lurch just out of sight.
If I cannot know my own mind,
Cannot fathom the reaches of my soul,
How is it that I lean on you so heavily?
I wish for dawn, the coming of the light,
So I can once more stand alone and try to see.

Listen, Listen

Listen for the silence
Underneath the whisper of the wind
Below the roar of the waves,
The shifting of the sand,
The screech of the seagulls,
Listen for the pounding of your heart.
Hear the mind's quiet searching
With every breath you take
Every wish for a tranquil day,
A happy night,
The awful longing for peace.
Listen, listen.

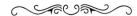

Dropped from the heavens

It is falling. White, soft fluffy bundles.
They pour down from a gloomy dark sky.
I did not want them.
I like walking on clear roads.
I like seeing the grass, even brown and dull.
I want the cars to go safely, no skidding.
No running into ditches.
No accidents.
But the sky did not ask for my opinion.
The drops accelerate.
Now it is so fast, so dense I cannot make out
The individual flakes
But am lost in a dense pattern of whirling white.
My mind cannot take in this cold madness.
Encasing, encompassing, massing, piling up around me.
Soon I will not be able to push my way through it.
Is it possible that one tiny drop of water can enforce so much,
give a strong world so much trouble? How can something
this small become so huge? Is it a metaphor for love?

Enigma

I was happy. That little thrill of joy at the sound of his voice
Running through me.
We talk of small things that seem important to us.
A cold that will not go away, a friend who has a problem,
Work with its up and downs.
I leave the phone with the sweet haze of love surrounding me.
The television calls to me, I turn it on
To utter horror.
Other people died while I was frittering away my life.
Another woman kissed her lover good-bye as she stood in line
To get the ticket that would take her on a trip.
A mother felt only joy as she started toward her son's wedding.
Bodies remain, the hopes, the plans, even this trip is gone,
Ended before it started.
What happened? Why? What have we done
to bring this anger down upon us?
I worry that we have made some big mistake
While we were living our small lives.
I fear that in our selfish happiness
We have let in to others some misery they cannot withstand
And we have not understood.

To love an ISIS

I never met an ISIS
For which mostly I am glad
But some days when I watch the news
I want to hug the mother of an ISIS man.
I want to put my arms around her and say it is alright.
We understand.
Altho I know we do not, nor does she.
Like me she brought out a son in an anguish soon forgotten,
The first cry, the first smile, love gushing forth.
So she told him stories, showed him the
ways that men must grow,
He learned so well, became a religious
man to make his father proud.
Now she is quiet as she sheds her tears.
They call him "Martyr", "Hero",
She calls him "son" as she recalls his childish days.
She does not understand the triumph that they praise
When all she feels is loss. She does not know
That another mother in a far off land can truly share her pain.

Joshua tree

I have not seen a Joshua tree
For several years now.
But I remember.
I have been brought down,
Bent and gnarled by the conquering strength
Of Shingles.
My limbs feel bent, my head constantly on fire,
My life constrained and lowered and bruised.
But like the Joshua tree, I still reach out.
I stretch my imperfect arms toward god
And feel the warm of sun, the cool of breeze,
I know that altho damaged, I have strength and
Inner beauty I can share.
So like the Joshua trees I live and reach for life.

Must be the air.

It is the air.
It must be the air.
It is the air.
I can scarcely feel it until the wind moves it.
But it must be the air, above the ocean,
over the lakes, across the fields,
Down from the mountains.
Where else cometh my strength?
Over and over life has proved itself too much for me.
I do not have the strength to bear the sorrows,
Cannot endure the anguish of the daily grinds,
No way can I rise above the agony of pain.
And yet I do.
And so do you.
The things we fear the most
Dwindle to inconsequence when we sit beside the bog,
Looking out over emptiness, watching
for the far ocean to gather itself
To come roaring in, filling the muddy flats with coolness
While over us all hovers the air.
It must be the air.
It is the air.

Impossible

Looks are so deceitful.
He looks so healthy, but he's not
He always picked the hardest way to live,
Hid in the closet of despair until AIDS forced him out
He tried to make amends, to warn the
world of the impending doom.
Spent sleepless nights telling his peers
A better, safer way to live and love.
Once when I was ill,
I saw him standing by my window
On the sill there were two plants
A Christmas cactus waved its brilliant fingers at him.
Next to it stood a prickly cactus, purely green.
Sharp and sober as a guard.
Even as I watched, he ran his fingers up the spiny bristles
Patting it lovingly, soothing it,
Ignoring the easy brilliance of the blossoming one.
This man, who always chose the cumbrous way,
Gives solace to lost souls, feeds puppies, vagrants,
Gives gifts of laughter, shelter, food to those the world rejects,
Sends the effortless beauty on its way,
Gives solace to the untouchable one.

My Amy

I taught in a school plopped down in the
middle of a housing project.
We saw it all reflected in the eyes of our children.
Amy was special,
Not more bedraggled or abused than the others.
But she had a special shine, like the first star
That comes out from behind a cloud.
She would come in dragging the cloud of injustice,
Standing reluctantly to pledge allegiance to the country
Which did not seem to be giving her the freedom she needed.
But as the day began she became the Amy I admired.
No wasting time chewing on pencils, making
paper hats, whispering to friends.
She threw herself into work.
If her first paper did not appear to be pristine,
She started another.
She read everything, had answers to teacher's questions
And had questions of her own.
She earned the name of "Teacher's pet" and rightly so
For who could not love that searching mind.
She left to go to middle school and soon I lost her
In the aftershock of new and different problem kids.
It was many years before we crossed paths again.
I taught, retired, and volunteered with the Salvation Army
Whose motto- "Doing the most good" seemed to ring true.
At a Christmas benefit I once again met Amy.
A whittled down, bedraggled Amy.
Reduced to begging for food, ashamed, defeated.
I recognized her still and threw my arms around her.
I asked her. "why did you not come to me?"
And she burst into tears.
"I didn't want you to know what had become of me"
She said through tears.
Eventually she told the story I did not want to hear.

My shining star lay in a gutter deep and dark.
She lived in a hotel where strangers paid her rent,
Using her body as commodity.
Meth had stolen all her teeth so now her smile
Only beseeched the lowest kind of man and was not real.
We gave her food and other Christmas things,
But though I offered my love and friendship,
She rejected me, the bit of pride that still remained was strong.
My Amy, just one more victim of our poverty.

New day

It is still dark
And I am huddled in my bed.
Long torn apart from restless dreams.
The sky is drawing light,
Moment by moment it pulls in shades of grey
And lets hope in, one silken ray at a time.
Reluctantly, I rise to watch out of my window.
Most fortunate of women, I have a view out toward
The hovering sea.
As light begins to force its timid way into the sky
I shiver at the shore, waiting.
Beyond belief, in comes another day.
Shimmering with hope, bright darts of golden promises
Slicing their way into the clouds. Hope
conquering all. It is a new and better day.
It must be better, for we need an answer to our prayers,
A thread of hope coming down through pastel dawns
Into the brilliant light of day.
Every night we leave concerns and travel to a resting place,
with dreams held safe in hidden places of our hearts,
Ready to be brought into the light of day when time is right.
Perhaps today will be that day.

No sink?

What if I couldn't afford a cleaning lady?
What if I couldn't clean the sink?
What if I didn't have a sink?
Foolish woman, how could that happen?
Ask the woman who stays most of the day in her tent
Singing softly to her child,
Pretending they are camping for fun
While her heart bleeds silently.
She is waiting for her husband who marched by foot
While she got a ride in a truck.
Fleeing her home, leaving her shining new home,
Leaving the job that her husband loved,
And the new kitchen with a lovely sink.
Leaving because her next door neighbor's home was bombed
And her husband's work place vanished into smoke
From bombardment.
She no longer worries about her house, her sink,
She only worries that he will find her,
That they will live through this and not
Sink.

On meeting God

Hello at last.
I know now why they say "Higher power",
It took me such a long time to get up here,
So many years of struggle.
Now that I am here I still cannot find what I need.
I have asked friendly angels, darling cherubs,
Even the harp player does not know.
"Where is the complaint department?"
For wondrous one, that gave me such gifts
That oftentimes my heart would glow,
Who put me down beside a rhythmic sea to calm my soul
And stimulate my mind,
There are mistakes made every day.
And God, I hate to be the one to tell you this,
But often they are made in your name.
I know how busy you are keeping all the stars aloft,
The trees from bending in the gale, the rivers in their beds.
I know making the mind of man receptive to beauty,
Must be a consuming task,
But please, Could you distribute Peace?

One blade

One tiny blade of grass.
Weak, slender, pale and yet it holds back a hill.
One meager stalk, where once there might have been a tree,
Will keep a landslide standing there.
Well, no, the blade alone is not omnipotent
but gathered with others
Exerts a strength that keeps the powerful sand at bay.
Gives it a reason to stay still, to do its job.
The grass unites to fill a landscape, give
us who only pass along the road
A glance of beauty, strength, the strength that nature bestows
On us, the simple passers by.
Alone we are so powerless, so fragile,
But gathered with nature's pure forces
we concentrate a strength
That keeps danger away, brings beauty to our day.
One blade of grass can calm a hill from sliding to the sea.
I wonder if one prayer can do the same for me?

Phases of life

Childhood is just a blur of love and fear
Youth is a flying, fragrant time.
Work and families move swiftly,
Occupying days and months
That slip by almost un-noticed,
Then wham- old age shows up.
It is not delicate in its approach.
For some it slides in with a simple loss of facilities.
For others it steals huge parts of abilities,
For others it sends in lightening bolts of illness.
To many of us it comes as a huge surprise,
We did not see that we were changing.
We felt no loss, until one day we looked in the mirror
To gasp as our mother's face looked back at us.
Perhaps then we noticed how we hesitate at stairs,
How we forget phone numbers, arise more reluctantly.
That is the time to join a club, take up a hobby long neglected.
Make new and younger friends, Forget
that time is asking for a toll.
We have paid up our dues and now it's time to watch
The gulls and learn to soar!!

Companions

I have heard it said that a poet's life
Is a lonely one.
But I do not find it so.
Since I awoke to my poet-ness
I have been surrounded.
At first it was noisy sea-gulls and pounding waves
That kept me company.
As I grew used to nature's quiet ways, I heard
Soft messages on errant breeze,
Loud messages called down from clouds of raging thunder,
And tiny whispers from emerging leaves.
As life stirs up and out from muddy flats
The air flutters with motion and breaths from those who hid
Below its depths in anticipation of renewal.
Trembling with joy at spring's first warming rays
The fragile roots of lily's shake themselves to rise again.
A woodpecker hears a sound beyond my ken,
And sends his pounding message through the woods.
The moss listens and takes the cue and begins to green.
A mayflower finds its strength and starts to lift its head.
An osprey, circling high, feels a strange urge,
And picks up a stray twig and drops it on its perch.
It sits a moment looking down on us, the earthbound ones,
To wonder what we see and what we do.
While I below, wish that I could soar like that.

Amazon's Bargain Book

For two cents--
Well, there is the postage added,
But I don't think of that
I can transport myself to 1558
And be a princess so in love nothing else matters.
I can read about a girl so lonely,
So lacking of love, although there are times when
She has a nation's adoration,
So madly in love with an ambitious man,
That she can think of nothing else.
She would gladly give up her throne in exchange
For a wedding ring, but that could not be.
So I suffer with her all the way,
Through losses and jealous scorn,
Through fear and nights of tears and loneliness,
I am no princess, have no crowds adoring me nor
Closets full of costly gowns and jewels.
But I can share with her the lonely nights,
The bursting dreams of love, the passion long unspent.
I can share with her the fear that he will be gone
And then, even the dream of love that sustains her
Will disappear.
And my own dream of love that seems as unlikely
As that of any queen may melt away
And I will be left just like Elizabeth,
A lonely girl.

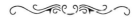

Angry world

The anger of this world has swallowed me.
I do not want to be an angry one --
But what else can we be in an angry world?
The whole world seems to be mad.
Our country used to be a haven of peace for immigrants
And now the children of those who came for safety
Are lining up to vote for an angry man for president.
He swears to build a wall high enough to keep everyone out.
Elitists say, "Oh, he is just a joke",
But he is not.
He stirs within us an anger we did not know we had,
An anger and a deeply hidden fear
That someone is going to take away our peace,
Our most fortunate lives where we can live in abundance,
Wander our roads fearless, eat too much,
partake of forbidden substances
And go our merry way while others pay a price
For tiny bits of freedom. At first I thought
it all a huge colossal joke
That would wind down and be blown away by other jokes.
But we are torches waiting to be lit, waiting
to find a place to vent our anger,
As the poor get poorer and the rich get richer
And we stand helpless wondering what to do.
So on our angers seethe while we stand helpless.

Prostrate

I lie upon the doorstep of hope
Grasping for one ray, one shaft of light.
The world swirls around me,
Dark and fearsome.
What is it that I wish for?
What do I want?
What do I fear?
Then faintly on an errant breeze
There comes the sound of angels voices,
A chorus breaks through.
A warm blanket covers my shaking shoulders.
Even as my body shudders
I feel the anguish drain away.
There is a golden warmth and I know Hope is there.
The beauty of a dawn crawls onto the horizon.
That is it.
The beauty of the world is brought to
me upon the wings of love.
I realize that since I love I am imbued with hope.

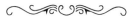

Snow bound

I was born in Vermont
Where for the first years I wondered
Why the adults spoke of the ground as green.
I only saw white, white soft snow that lay gentle on your head,
White hard snow that made men groan and grouch
As they shovel paths for us to walk upon.
Then one day --It must have been a July 4th--
I saw green buds poke through and for
a wondrous month or two
I saw green grass.
Where lambs could graze and flowers push through,
Where croquet sets grew rampant.
I understood the melody of green grass and forgot about white.
Until the wind grew harsh, the night dropped in earlier,
And down it came.
Flake by flake it brought back the ground I knew.
So soon I could forget the music of green grass,
Lie down in my familiar bed of snow and make an angel.
Now it has been years since I made angels,
where white means sheets
On beds, papers to be signed.
Until last night in utter silence came new snow,
Covering the streets, sign posts and lawns.
Each blade of grass absorbing its due share,
And I, a child again, lost in the wonder of it's beauty
Could once again walk on white.

Somedays

Somedays I feel that I am a drop of snow.
Just one little drop that falls down, white and lovely,
Perhaps meant to decorate a tree but instead
Falls on a moving, warm car and melts.
Almost before it has lived, it dies.
Before it has even known its destiny it is gone.
As I could be.
But other days I am the one small drop that lands
With others on a wire.
It finds the vital wire that keeps the world humming.
The extra weight of that small flake
Stops everything.
No light, no power, no communication.
The world lies prostrate at the feet of one small,
Melting drop that could be me.

The poetry of our lives

The social worker who came to my house yesterday
To keep me from becoming case number two zillion
In the annuals of old ladies who fell off the
cliff talked with me about my writing.
I showed her 3 poems I had written.
She said, "I could never have done these"
No. My head is telling me.
She could not.
But neither could I have used the skills she used to calm me,
Involve me in different thoughts, straighten out a mess
In my house, which indirectly straightened out my head.
We are each as unique as a snow flake,
Sometimes as useless.
Drifting aimlessly, melting at the first ray of sun,
Or piling up until we become a problem.
We are so different in shape and aim and posture.
We land in different places, insert our lives in various ways,
Until like a melted snowflake we are a part of the landscape.
Then in the sequence of the days,
The silence of the nights, our lives exert their own abilities,
Each of us moving to a different rhythm,
learning our own rhymes.
Every life a story,
And we, the story tellers, expressing
ourselves through our actions.
For some of us life is a sonnet, others write limericks.
To one life is free verse, changing with the days,
To others just an ode to what was done.
Each of us writes with a free hand, reaching
out to use the talent that we have
And try to share the melody.

This vision came to me.

God sent it down under cover of darkness.
I have never been in such a place. But I can feel it.
My heart is torn and I doubt if it will mend
Because while I live in a peaceful place,
Deluged by gifts of things. A peaceful morning. followed
by a quiet day of food and friends and work for pay.
But by the same sea in another land a girl is sitting sobbing.
Her face still streaked with tears, she has become determined.
With a stick she scratches in the dirt.
She makes the figure of a man. It must be a man,
Faceless and tall, exuding strength.
She weeps as she finishes, then looks around for a bigger stick.
She finds one only steps away, returns and
smashes, smashes, pounds until there is no
more face, no more body, no more man.
Only a large dent in the sand and a tiny weeping girl
who does not know where to go.

Child of ISIS

What is it like to be a child of ISIS?
To have a quiet, attentive mother, who holds you close
When your father leaves to go to work?
Perhaps he gives her a perfunctory kiss as he leaves,
Perhaps he pats you on the head as he departs.
Does that child know that as his father properly does his job
He ends someone else's dreams?
As he wins praise, both here and in a future life,
Another life is ended, and with it the many tentacles that love
Promotes. Do children of ISIS feel their fathers triumph
At a job well done? Is that how the next generation is formed?
Where does that leave us?
What is it like to be a child of America?
To have a quiet attentive mother, who holds you close
When your father leaves to go to work?

Whispers

The wind whispers
The water sparkles
Tears fall.
The days come and go, almost un-noticed
Until suddenly a birthday comes
To make you take stock of how much time
Has disappeared.
Life has been moving on without your will,
Just living easily on the flow
Of rainy nights and foggy days,
Rejoicing in the sun when it appears.
There is an urgency that whispers softly,
"Hurry. Go.
Make the most of these most precious days."
For we are among the lucky ones
That only hear the whispers of impending dooms.
The bursts of gun-fire seldom reach our ears.
The greatest losses of our days
Are monetary, age and sickness.
We have escaped the fate of half the world
That sleeps in violence and wakes to watch
Destruction of antiquity.
So easily torn down are structures
Long ago others gave up their lives to build.
Beauty gives up with just a sigh
Before the hammers of hate,
While all the time the sea goes on
And few listen to the whispers of the wind.

White waves

White waves upon the water,
Yesterday the ocean pushed small waves upon the sand
So inviting.
I put my feet into the water
And withdrew them fast.
It is April and although the tulips bloom
The cold has lingered in the water.
As I pulled back I heard the ocean laugh.
That laughter followed me as I trekked home.
Nature has its own agenda.
It does not watch a calendar or listen
To the weather man.
The soft green moss has made its path inviting too
But it does not mean the cold is gone.
The trees begin to bud and fruit will blossom as it wills.
We can stand near the blueberry bush
Encouraging it with words.
While it smiles sweetly and takes its time
To bring its berries to our mouths.
The ocean has its own strong will
When waves may lap upon the shore or roar
With white froth pounding on our rocks.
In years another human will bend down
To pick up a pebble from this shore,
Admire it and wonder from where it came.
The ocean, having done its work, may withdraw
To have its laugh in secret.

Wise?

How wonderful that in old age He lets you know
A lot of things that used to be mysterious.
He must be a funny guy, laughing alone
In the great here-after.
Saying to himself, "Why not let her in on some
of the secrets? Even if she tells, who would believe her?"
So here I am, a little senile perhaps, but definitely old.
Seeing a lot and seeing through a lot and remembering
Consequences, and how they came about.
But no one wants to know.
Each one of us wants to make our own paths.
Unlike the dogs who sniff out every one
who marked this trail before.
Who is the wiser?

Speak out

In a world where we are afraid.
Intelligent people afraid to turn on the TV
Wise people turning directly to the crossword puzzle.
The rest is too scary to read,
We feel so hopeless.
But we have a powerful weapon we can turn on the world.
We need to learn how to bring down the clouds of words
Hovering in the broad skies of our minds,
Lose the thunderbolts, dodge the rain.
We want the community of man, of ordinary people,
The salt of our earth, to be seen and heard and even tasted.
We want to remind the world that we are truly what matters.
That names of political groups will be forgotten in history,
The battles one more fact to lodge in memory.
But it is the people that will go on.
Docile workhorses who obey their minority leaders,
Or strong vigilantes who make their own way.
Who survives will depend on when and how and where
We raise our voices.
Not our guns, our voices.

Meditation

I put my feet firmly on the ground
Lord knows I could use grounding
Especially now
When the murmur of your name inside my head
Sends me soaring.
I fold my restless hands upon my lap and close my eyes.
I stand on the edge of a volcano
Looking down into a blaze of crimson.
I see flames, I feel heat—
Oh, the heat –
But I'm afraid to go there.
I stand beside the ocean.
The sand sparkles with diamonds.
I scurry around,
Grasping for gold, the jewels, diamonds in the sun
Eluding my grasp, fading before my touch.
I see night approaching. I see the egrets start their flight
To shelter in the trees.
I know that I need shelter too
Before the stars come out to drop their magic on my eyes.
I know that I
Have nowhere else to go but you.

Flower

So tenderly, so frail
It pokes through the ground
Looking wounded, looking frightened.
A tiny seed still on its tip, slender stalk holding it
Wavering as if to ask
"Where am I?"
I here its fragile voice asking,
"Is this where I belong?"
Ah little would-be flower
How well I know your quandary. I too have asked that question.
I guess we blossom where we were planted,
Or merely dropped. But this is where we are
So we must raise these drooping heads,
Seek out the sun and learn to thrive.
I look at you, so fragile and so weak and see
The flower you will grow to be.

Thoughts about love

Sometimes I think love is a pain in the neck
As well as other places.
It means going places you didn't want to go.
Being polite to people you really don't like,
Embracing in-laws that look at you scornfully.
It means saying dinner was delicious, when it wasn't.
Agreeing to see the movie you said you'd never watch.
But it also means having someone to watch the sunrise with.
It means laughing at a joke nobody else gets.
Sometimes it is wiping up tears no-one else saw,
Or taking the blame for something someone else did.
It can be funny, hysterical, laughter inducing
Or it can be serious, tragic and hurtful.
Until it is gone,
No-one seems to know
How important it was.

Piece on Earth

Somewhere there must be just a little piece of earth
That could belong to me.
I read of gardens green and flowering,
I hear of mountains planted with tall trees.
I know that food flows out from fertile plantings
Gathering nourishment from the dark ground
To fill our hungry mouths
But what will ease my hungry soul?
I started out on wobbly, spindly legs
That grew stronger with time,
Legs that have tread a dusty path and taken me too many miles
Yet nowhere that I can call my own.
Even the country that I once thought of as mine
No longer seems to belong to me.
Political people claim to conquer it even
as sunsets roll across the sky
New days bring only barbed barriers to keep me out.
My only shelter holds within my mind where there must be
A kind of respite built of hope that somewhere there is
A little piece of ground that will belong to me.

Love

I do not know if I can do this.
These wild emotions rock me, twist me, turn
My faltering heart around.
Until it wants to burst from this frail body
And soar into the sky like the gulls I have so long admired.
I want to stand somewhere upon a hill,
A mountaintop, a cloud
Screaming to the world-
I found him.
I found love or it found me.
When I had given up, ready to fade away into oblivion
He came, unbidden into my quiet life and turned it all around.
Now I cannot live long enough, sing loud enough,
Or stretch my heart enough.

Rapture

I am floating on the ether of your love.
A moment ago I walked the earth, pigeon like, mundane
One touch, one fragile moment and I flew.
The days of yearning, watching as gulls rose
Spreading their wings to cover all the ordinary world
Are gone. For now, at last
Lifted by love I see the silver sea, the golden shine of dunes.
I feel the caress of the air, lifting me, embracing me, holding me.
One touch to last me all my life.
If never again your hand reaches mine
I still have lived, have flown, have known rapture enough
To last me all my days.

Broken Shell

There you are, broken on the beach,
A small brown entity curled around
your core as if for protection.
You call to me until I stoop to pick you up.
Nestled in my hand I see the fragility and the strength.
For I have also been a broken shell.
Times were when I huddled around myself
As there did not seem to be sustenance elsewhere.
But I have been saved by love.
No longer frightened of the many flaws, the chips,
The unfilled curve that ends nowhere.
Perhaps you too, knowing the beauty you once had is changed
But seen by someone who joins and loves you,
Perhaps you too will know your life goes on.

Cracked

The past rides heavy on my heart tonight
The past will not stay buried where it lies.
The childhood fears show through again
The trembling legs, the shortened breath.
The darkest clouds roll out from fear
through the crevasses
Of walls my mind has built.
For a minute I'm afraid, before I see
That where fissures have ripped apart
There comes a ray of light.
Brightening the dullest cloud
The silver lining starts to glow.
At last the sky begins to lighten,
There is nothing left to truly frighten.
The past is over, gone away.
The future is here to stay.
The beauty of the world endures
As yesterday is swallowed by today.

Sand

I saw a speck upon the sand today
Colorless, sparkling, diving in and out
among the other sands
It hid a moment, then dashed back
First hiding shyly, then displaying.
It made me think of you.
How slowly I had let your ashes dribble from my finger-tips
How softly they slid in to mingle with the other particles
How separate they stayed
How once lost they could never be retrieved
Each moment of our lives, separate and mingled,
Each apart but joined
Once lost could never be rejoined.
But hidden in the sands of time
Washed ever by the waves of memory
Kept glowing by the memory of love
Upon the shore of life.

Pretentious Gull

Pretentious gull
Striding along in front of me
Head high, chest out.
I see your sidewise glance,
How you only pretend to ignore me.
I know you stride a bit precociously.
Wanting to tell me just to look.
Knowing that you can do the thing I long to do.
Knowing that with a short run you can take off
And see the world below you
While I can only wish.
But, gull, you do not know
That I have found the secret.
That on the wings of love I too can fly.
I too can see the whole world through a clearer eye
Than I have ever felt before.
Soaring on the strength of someone else's love
I too can conquer everything
And float in bliss.
Move over, gull, for there is room for two.

Equilibrium

The whole world could go to hell in a basket
As it seems to be prone to doing,
And we wouldn't care.
Together we could be happy,
Living on air and Blueberry pie
And love.

Awakening

I woke up the morning today.
Sat on the stairs leading down to the water
Surrounded by mist and cool breeze
The water lapped softly against the grey sand
Under a grey lonely sky.
I asked it again and again
What was it trying to tell me?
What secret does the sea hold
That it is trying to share?
The duck floating by so serenely
Has he known the story long?
Does the gull laughing loudly
At a joke I didn't hear
Know the enigma as well?
So I asked it again and again.
Do I have to wait until I join the ocean,
Until my life is rejoined to the sea
To understand what we are here for,
What the mystery is all about.
Just as I finally asked my question,
As I gathered myself to stand and leave
Morning awoke in a great gulp
Sunlight broke through, scattering clouds
Like broken balloons.
The earth clutched the rays until sand
Brought out diamonds to proudly display
Seaweed turned magnificent colors
A myriad of greens, blacks and browns
Showing me shades I'd never seen.
Sea glass shimmered, shells began to move,
Out of the mist came a grandeur,

A brilliance of future and past.
Once again the gull laughed.
Don't you know he seemed to ask
The answers are already here.

Distance

Sometimes when I am computing words of love
To someone who lives far from me
I think.
Sometimes I feel the mother who kissed
Beloved children tenderly, saying "Have a good life"
And turned away to hide her tears,
For never could she brave the ocean waves in leaky boats
To wander far from land she could not leave behind.
We are so fortunate now that with the tap of a finger
We can bring the words, the sight, even the voice, of ones
We will not see again in person.
No distance is too far, no change too great,
We still can stay in touch as much as the heart will allow.
It is a strange thing that our innermost thoughts, our loves,
Desires and fears in order to be shared by loved ones
Must be tossed out upon the air where privacy is just a concept
Here the baring of the soul is in the open,
Could be pirated away by anyone who
hacked their way into my life.
Not that my life is quite that special, except to me.
But what I say to you is meant for you alone.
The men who made these methods of connection,
Did they concern themselves with privacy? Is it safe
For me to tell the world the secrets that I meant for you alone.
Perhaps I worry needlessly?

Last argument

He lies upon a battle field screaming at God.
Poor boy he was.
His mother said, "Why not try out the army for a bit.
Perhaps things will be different when you come back".
He tries to state his case.
"I haven't lived yet. I wasted all that time on booze and girls.
Give me another chance."
But God shakes his head, the thunder rolls.
God says "I have to hurry up. Another storm is coming.
But I will save your days. I'll give your days to that old lady
Who is just finding her way. I think she needs them."
So He does.
Now here I am, spending the days that lost boy left.
What do I do?
Where do I go?
Can I make him live?

Terrorist

How do I dare to think you are like me?
If I found you starving on the street could
I share my sandwich with you?
If your lips were parched could I lift water to your lips?
I do not dare.
I do not dare to think you are like me.
It is difficult enough to think that we
must share our world with you.
The very air we breathe seems polluted by your fury.
I do not want my son to visit your land, beautiful as it is.
I fear he might invoke your rage.
I would not let him in the lion's den and yet I could pet a tiger
More easily then I could touch you.
The anger in an animals dark eyes is not as viral as is yours.
The veneer of humanity which cloaks your
animosity is wearing through.
I fear the fierceness of the hatred I see blazing in your face
But fear more truly the fervor I feel rising in my chest
I am afraid that touching your violence might ignite the fire
Of vengeance I feel festering in me
So I try to look at the sky that hovers over both of us,
Watch for the stars that brighten both our skies, feel the rain
That moistens our dry skin, pray for
forgiveness that we both have hate.

No answer

The world is aflame and we poets write of beauty.
Of birds flying and trees blooming and the ocean flowing calm.
While men steal girls to sell for moneys sake
And innocent boys grab guns and hurry off to right the wrongs
That older voices told them needed fixing.
Fathers sit helpless, wringing useless hands
When every morning women look at empty beds and weep.
That bed may be only a bedroll in an empty corner
But the pain is just as deep and the loss—
The terrible losses no one can count—
Go into eternity.
The boy who stood on the brink of a medical breakthrough,
The girl whose voice could have thrilled concert halls,
The child who healed a thousand days of suffering
By dropping just one kiss upon his mother's forehead.
Children fight, partners argue, countries war.
How can we end it? Should we sing better songs?
Is it time to quell our fears and sing of war?

Worker bees

We have named them all,
The many men the town has sent to do a two-man job.
There is the Leaner –he who leans for hours against his shovel,
The Watcher – he who watches the Leaner,
There is the Super –Watcher, whose main
job seems to be watching those two.
There is the one who actually shovels
He is the Shoveler.
There are a couple, one who seems to be in charge of jokes.
He is The Joker and the men all laugh a lot when he is active.
There is the Machine Man who never
puts a foot upon the ground,
Just keeps the machine running until
they get around to needing it.
Then there are police just in case a terrorist gets lost
And passes all the street closed signs.
But my favorite is the Kicker. He sits in
The machine until needed.
Then he walks behind the truck. Raises his
leg and gives the truck one swift kick.
Job done.

On the back of the wind

On the back of the wicked wind comes spring
As he gallops over the land
I see her riding on his back,
Hair blowing, eyes laughing,
"Come on," she says
"One last puff.
Blow hard so when I come they truly
Will appreciate me.
My daffodils and violets slowly waking up
To push their way into the waiting land.
Sun sending down it's heat to warm those weary bones.
Give it one last ferocious thrust.
Then you can rest, take your time, enjoy my rosy blooms.
A little summer waft to remind us will be enough."

Love letter to the world

World I love you so much.
Not just the wonderful people,
The warmth of their smiles, the depth of their tears,
The amazing minds that bring up miracles of thought each day.
But the quiet influx of nature.
The way the sun rises in the morning, sending courage, vision,
Hope, upon its golden shafts.
The way the wind caresses you on a summer day
And wrenches tears from your eyes on freezing winter outings.
The predictability of summer—
It will come we tell ourselves
Each perilous spring.
Then come the frail sprouts
Rendering the fragile snowdrop of a flower
A lady slipper underneath the watchful eye of a birch tree.
A red-wing blackbird gamboling on a deserted picnic table.
The brook that ambles slowly until spring
When it runs gushing over rocks turning them silver
As it wanders toward
The ocean.
There lies our source of strength.
Beautiful on a sunny day, fierce in a storm,
Sending one wave after the other
As predictable as day itself.
When we are powerless
It lends its sovereignty
For us to sit upon its shore and gather in.
The ocean has enough to share.
In deep relaxing we can join the tempo of time
Becoming one more part of a universe
We cannot fathom

I hope the sages know
So that when I must leave there is a place
Where I can still be a part
Of this world I love so much.

Are we but one?

He hears the feet stomping in the barn.
He opens his eyes to a grey day and
wonders if the cows are cold.
Then he thinks of those whose hearts are cold.
She bends over a fussing baby, wishes she had a better place
To keep him warm and thriving and then
her mind goes to a kneeling boy
In a far off land drawing his last frightened breathe.
I think of turning up my thermostat
As years have made me frail enough to mind the cold
But I think of mothers and grandmothers living in shelters,
Walking sandy roads, the only water running from their eyes,
As they leave terror along with their
possessions in a place called home.
What do we have in common?
Only that we all are human. We all breathe
and bleed and love and fear.
We worry about those we love, try to help our neighbors,
Try to mind our own business.
But suddenly now it is our business.
A line of men whose names we do not
know are kneeling in the sand
Of a place we do not know, guarded by men we cannot know.
Men wielding swords, or guns, or lethal hands
And suddenly our hearts are breaking.
For it is us. We are the helpless, the fearful, the dying.
We are the ones who kneel at terrors door, obeying evil men
Who think they are gods with knowledge
and right at their disposal.
This world, that yesterday seemed beautiful and hopeful.
These people that yesterday seemed promising and creative,
We, who thought we had the answers,
are kneeling in our hearts,
Reeling in our minds. We only think revenge. We cannot live

With this outrage. But how and where? Who are these men?
Where are their families? Who loves
them? Where did they spawn?
Are these our brothers? Are we but one?

Favorite things

Clouds. They hover above, spoiling picnic
days making us scurry for shelter,
Put away summer foods, dash our hopes for a campfire.
But they also fill the air on a hot summer day
Allowing us to see whales swimming across the sky,
Castles, and forests, and tall ships as well.
They allow dreams to seem possible, lies to seem true.
Mud. Cool and murky it lies at the edge of the bog.
Step in and you ruin a good shoe, sink to your ankles in slime.
But sitting near the edge you hear
movement, the squeak of a bug,
The throb of a frog. Although silence
prevails there is a strange warmth,
A kind of inclusion, as though ready or
not, you are part of this world.
So when day ends and you watch the sun go down
It is clouds that enhance the magic of sunset.
The colors that flash from their edges, changing their shape,
Drawing out intensity, illuminating the darkness.
Perhaps it might be the clouds that show us the light?

Strangers

The wonderful love that brought us together
When we were yet strangers
Has been working a silent magic for years.
As I read poems you wrote in the past
And see poems that I wrote yesterday
I see the differences and the sameness.
You are younger, but wiser,
Your words sometimes stronger
And sometimes more hard to compute,
But me, simple and open
Can say the same thing in humble terms;
Interpreting the complex into easy knowledge.
We both ask forgiveness for mistakes we did not mean to make,
We both ask understanding of issues too complex to take,
Together we ask for God's blessing, your understanding,
strength from the ocean. The rivers, the sky.
It is comforting to me to see that when I lose my way
There is someone with strength to guide me.
We both end our letters with love.

Gift

I rather thought that if I gave you all my love
I would be left derelict, loveless.
Turns out it is not true.
The more I give more bubbles up
From an unknown stream of joy hidden
In depths I had not recognized.
The more that love flows out, more happiness flows in
The heart has resources not known to us,
A calling down from the bright stars blinking in dark skies,
Sliding in on the winter wind,
Slipping in silently upon each drop of snow,
Rising from the sweetest tones of music.
It crowds in, escaping from the chatter of the squirrels,
The chirping of the birds, the drilling of the woodpecker.
Renewed each morning in the gold of rising sun
Lasting until the silver of the moon takes over.
It seems, the more you give
The more you get.

Light

I cannot believe that love brings so much light.
Outside my window all is black.
The sky has no streaks of color,
The air is full of indiscernible mist,
But here in my dark room
There is a light.
Born blind, at last I see what love has brought to me.
So much I could not understand has been made clear
While much that I can never understand
Remains the sweetest melody.
How is it you, a creature so immense in wisdom, love, creativity
Could stoop to raise a foundering soul like me?
But I have no real need to find the answer
For it has happened.
At last I have been made true, a person with a dream
That can be reached,
A place to put my heart where it is safe,
A place to grow beside you all the way, learning, trusting
Standing erect in body and in soul because your arm
Around me gives me strength and leads me to the light.

There is a log in the woods

There is a log in the woods
Where my life stays when I am not using it.
Much of the time I leave it there.
I waste my day in platitudes and pleasures.
I let my legs carry me from place to place
Just being, not thinking.
My heart, these days, belongs to someone else,
So I no longer have to worry about that
And years have worn out fears and some desires.
I have no swords to sharpen, no races to be run,
Never another test to ace or flunk
For I have reached my goal.
I live where I want, love feverishly and wild.
See everything but keep it close, the keeper of others secrets
And my own desires.
As the golden sun sets into the ocean
So my own golden days settle into the bog
Where I return to fetch my life back from the log.

Mist

Mist, you are indeed mysterious.
I have been so lonely.
Alone or in a crowd, I have been so lonely.
No voice, no touch, have reached me.
Words from the ones I love most have not healed me.
So when I look out of a window to see day break over the bay
And see only mist
I am not surprised. That is my life.
Shrouded in darkness, filled with tears like rain,
Hovering above a perilous sea.
I watch the sky move, change. Allow a glint of yellow, pink,
Then orange. How it moves.
My body stirs, or is it just my soul?
Fear stirs as well, tries to initiate a place, draws back
When to my startled heart comes courage,
Wrapping me in a warmth I had not felt.
The soft patter of mist removes the vestiges of doubt.
Every drop of mist is filled with future.
Here comes the sun.

ABC

Yes, lovely world
We are together, you and I.
Each day dawns new and fragile
Ready to open doors as we open our eyes
But even as the light comes in so does the wind.
At first a breeze that lifts the tendrils of our hair
In gentleness, becomes a torrent, then a gale
While we sit wondering where we should go,
What is our role, how should we move?
Are we the passive players here
Or do we really own this world?
Do we control our destiny
Or are we boughs that bend and sway
In the whim of the wild wind?

Winter song

Ah, little birdie how you sing!
The depths of winter hanging low over your tree,
The boughs bent low by icy snow
You raise your head
And liquid fire flames out
The ice around our hearts melts
While the tree maintains its stoic pose
But you, the tiniest fragment on the tree
Pour out your hope,
Your cheery song that says
The winter may be long and cold
But we survived and life is good.
Ah, little birdie, how you sing.

Sunset

How quietly our little lives slip past
One hand clasp at a time.
The smile that lit the morning leaves by noon
Another day ends with a yawn.
To begin again with a glancing blow from a sun
That disappears behind a cloud.
The love that seemed a miracle at birth
Becomes a burden holding on
To memories that twinge and pain.
The sun sinks softly into the sea
With a gasp of color lighting the whole sky
For just a moment.

This is tomorrow

I used to watch the sunset.
The glorious colors paint the sky,
As with a shudder the sun leaves
And I would cry.
"Tomorrow", said my peers.
"Tomorrow will be better."
Now it is here. This is tomorrow.
Those first faint rays
Like petals pushing from a stem
Flower across a gloomy sky.
A gleam of gold, the palest pink,
The cry of a lone bird.
Then here it comes—
The light, the light.
It is indeed tomorrow.

Edwards Brothers Malloy
Thorofare, NJ USA
July 27, 2016